Pies

igloobooks

Published in 2015
by Igloo Books Ltd
Cottage Farm
Sywell
NN6 0BJ
www.igloobooks.com

Food photography and recipe development: PhotoCuisine UK
Front and back cover images © PhotoCuisine UK

HUN001 0615
4 6 8 10 9 7 5 3
ISBN 978-1-78343-457-2

Printed and manufactured in China

Contents

Classic Pies

Beef and potato lattice pies

Makes: 6

Preparation time: 1 hour

Cooking time: 25 minutes

Ingredients

225 g / 8 oz / 1 ¼ cups potatoes, sliced

300 g / 10 ½ oz / 2 cups
   sirloin steak, sliced

4 tbsp butter, softened

1 clove of garlic, crushed

1 tbsp dill, chopped

For the pastry

400 g / 14 oz / 2 ⅔ cups plain
   (all purpose) flour

200 g / 7 oz / ¾ cup butter, cubed
   and chilled

1 egg, beaten

Method

To make the pastry, sieve the flour into a mixing bowl then rub in the butter until the mixture resembles fine breadcrumbs. Stir in just enough cold water to bring the pastry together into a pliable dough. Chill for 30 minutes.

Meanwhile, parboil the potatoes in salted water for 10 minutes, then drain well.

Preheat the oven to 200°C (180°C fan) / 400F / gas 6. Roll out half of the pastry on a floured surface and cut out 6 circles then use them to line 6 tartlet tins.

Divide half of the potatoes between the cases, then top with the steak before finishing with a layer of potatoes. Beat the butter with the garlic and dill, then dot it over the top of the potatoes.

Roll out the rest of the pastry and cut out 6 circles for the lids. Lay them on top of the pastry cases and crimp the edges to seal. Re-roll the trimmings and cut the sheet into 1 cm (½ in) strips. Lay them on top of the pies in a lattice pattern, then brush the tops with beaten egg.

Bake the pies for 25 minutes or until the pastry is cooked underneath and golden brown on top.

Creamy chicken and leek pie

Serves: 4

Preparation time: 30 minutes

Cooking time: 45 minutes

Ingredients

2 tbsp butter

2 leeks, sliced

1 tbsp plain (all purpose) flour

250 ml / 9 fl. oz / 1 cups milk

3 cooked chicken breasts, cubed

150 ml / 5 ½ fl. oz / ⅔ cup crème fraiche

½ tsp freshly grated nutmeg

2 tbsp tarragon, finely chopped

450 g / 1 lb / 2 cups all-butter puff pastry

1 egg, beaten

salt and pepper

Method

Heat the butter in a saucepan and fry the leeks for 10 minutes without colouring. Sprinkle in the flour and stir well, then stir in the milk and bubble until it thickens. Add the chicken and crème fraiche and heat through, then season to taste with salt and white pepper. Stir in the nutmeg and tarragon, then leave to cool completely.

Preheat the oven to 200°C (180°C fan) / 400F / gas 6.

Roll out half the pastry on a lightly floured surface and use it to line a pie dish. Spoon in the filling and level the top, then brush round the rim with water. Roll out the rest of the pastry and lay it over the top then trim away any excess.

Brush the top of the pie with beaten egg then bake for 45 minutes or until the pastry is cooked through underneath and golden brown on top.

Pork, carrot and sage pie

Serves: 4

Preparation time: **45 minutes**

Cooking time: **40 minutes**

Ingredients

2 tbsp olive oil

300 g / 10 ½ oz / 2 cups pork shoulder, cubed

1 onion, chopped

1 large carrot, peeled, and chopped

1 tsp dried sage

1 tbsp plain (all purpose) flour

1 tbsp concentrated tomato purée

500 ml / 18 fl. oz / 2 cups chicken stock

For the pastry

200 g / 7 oz / 1 cup butter, cubed, and chilled

400 g / 14 oz / 2 ⅔ cups plain (all purpose) flour

Method

First make the pastry. Rub the butter into the flour until the mixture resembles fine breadcrumbs. Stir in just enough cold water to bring the pastry together into a pliable dough then chill for 30 minutes.

Meanwhile, heat the butter in a saucepan and fry the onion and carrot for 5 minutes without colouring. Add the pork and sear on all sides to seal. Sprinkle in the flour and stir well, then stir in the tomato purée, sage and stock and bubble until it thickens. Leave to cool completely.

Preheat the oven to 200°C (180°C fan) / 400F / gas 6.

Roll out half the pastry on a lightly floured surface and use it to line a pie dish. Spoon in the filling and level the top, then brush round the rim with water.
Roll out the rest of the pastry and lay it over the top. Trim away any excess, then crimp round the edge with your thumb and forefinger. Prick the top to allow the steam to escape.

Bake the pie for 40 minutes or until the pastry is cooked through underneath and golden brown on top.

Potato pie

Serves: 6

Preparation time: 30 minutes

Cooking time: 45 minutes

Ingredients

450 g / 1 lb / 2 ½ cups potatoes, peeled
   and sliced
1 clove of garlic, crushed
300 ml / 10 ½ fl. oz / 1 ¼ cups double
   (heavy) cream
2 tbsp tarragon, finely chopped
450 g / 1 lb / 2 cups all-butter puff pastry
1 egg, beaten
salt and pepper

Method

Preheat the oven to 200°C (180°C fan) / 400F / gas 6.

Parboil the potatoes in salted water for 10 minutes, then drain well. Toss the potatoes with the garlic, cream and tarragon and season well with salt and pepper, then leave to cool to room temperature.

Roll out half the pastry on a floured surface and use it to line a pie dish. Pack the potatoes in tightly and pour over any cream left in the bowl.

Roll out the rest of the pastry and lay it over the top then crimp the edges to seal. Trim away any excess pastry and make a hole in the top for the steam to escape. Score a pattern in the top, being careful not to cut all the way through, then brush the top with beaten egg.

Bake the pie in the oven for 45 minutes or until the pastry is cooked through underneath and golden brown on top.

Salmon and dill pie

Serves: 6

Preparation time: 15 minutes

Cooking time: 40 minutes

Ingredients

450 g / 1 lb / 2 cups all-butter puff pastry

450 g / 1 lb / 3 cups skinless boneless salmon fillet, cubed

300 ml / 10 ½ fl. oz / 1 ¼ cups double (heavy) cream

1 tbsp Dijon mustard

2 egg yolks, beaten

2 tbsp dill, chopped

1 egg, beaten

salt and pepper

Method

Preheat the oven to 200°C (180°C fan) / 400F / gas 6.

Roll out half the pastry on a floured surface and use it to line a pie dish. Arrange the salmon on top in an even layer.

Mix the cream with the mustard, egg yolks, and dill and season with salt and white pepper, then pour it over the salmon.

Roll out the rest of the pastry and lay it on top. Trim away any excess and crimp round the edge, then brush it with beaten egg.

Bake the pie for 40 minutes or until the pastry is cooked through underneath and golden brown on top.

Mince and potato pie

Serves: 8

Preparation time: 45 minutes

Cooking time: 45 minutes

Ingredients

450 g / 1 lb / 2 ½ cups potatoes, peeled
   and sliced
2 tbsp olive oil
1 onion, finely chopped
1 medium carrot, sliced
2 cloves of garlic, finely chopped
450 g / 1 lb / 3 cups minced beef
½ tbsp fresh thyme leaves

For the pastry

400 g / 14 oz / 2 ⅔ cups plain
   (all purpose) flour
200 g / 7 oz / ¾ cup butter,
   cubed and chilled
1 egg, beaten

Method

To make the pastry, sieve the flour into a mixing bowl,
then rub in the butter until the mixture resembles fine
breadcrumbs. Stir in just enough cold water to bring
the pastry together into a pliable dough, then chill for
30 minutes.

Meanwhile, parboil the potatoes in a large pan of salted
water for 8 minutes, then drain well.

Heat the oil in a large frying pan and fry the onion,
carrot, and garlic for 5 minutes without colouring.
Add the minced beef and stir-fry for 5 minutes or until
it starts to brown. Leave to cool.

Preheat the oven to 200°C (180°C fan) / 400F / gas 6
and line a deep pie tin with greaseproof paper. Roll
out half the pastry on a floured surface and use it to line
the tin. Layer up the potatoes with the mince mixture
inside, then moisten the edge of the pastry with a little
water.

Roll out the rest of the pastry and lay it over the top
then trim away any excess pastry and crimp around the
edge with a fork. Make a hole in the top for the steam to
escape before brushing with beaten egg.

Bake the pie for 45 minutes or until the pastry is cooked
through underneath and golden brown on top.

Fish pie

Serves: 6

Preparation time: 30 minutes

Cooking time: 40 minutes

Ingredients

500 ml / 17 ½ fl. oz / 2 cups milk

1 bay leaf

200 g / 7 oz / smoked haddock fillet

4 tbsp butter

2 tbsp plain (all purpose) flour

200 g / 7 oz / 1 ⅓ cups skinless
   boneless salmon fillet, cubed

150 g / 5 ½ oz / 1 cup raw
   king prawns, peeled

2 tbsp dill, chopped

450 g / 1 lb / 2 cups all-butter puff pastry

1 egg, beaten

salt and pepper

Method

Put the milk and bay leaf in a small saucepan and bring to a simmer. Lay the haddock in a snugly fitting dish and pour the hot milk over the top. Cover the dish with cling film and leave to stand for 10 minutes.

Heat the butter in a small saucepan and stir in the flour. Strain in the haddock milk, stirring constantly. Cook until the sauce is thick and smooth.

Remove any skin and bones from the haddock, then flake the flesh into the white sauce and stir in the salmon, prawns and dill. Season to taste with salt and black pepper and leave to cool.

Preheat the oven to 200°C (180°C fan) / 400F / gas 6.

Roll out half the pastry on a floured surface and use it to line a baking dish. Spoon in the filling and level the top.

Roll out the rest of the pastry and lay it on top. Trim away any excess and crimp round the edge. Use the offcuts to decorate the top, then brush it with beaten egg.

Bake the pie for 40 minutes or until the pastry is cooked through underneath and golden brown on top.

Lamb, pea and mint pie

Serves: 4

Preparation time: **30 minutes**

Cooking time: **30 minutes**

Ingredients

2 tbsp olive oil

450 g / 1 lb / 3 cups minced lamb

1 onion, finely chopped

3 cloves of garlic, finely chopped

600 ml / 1 pint / 2 ½ cups good quality
   beef stock

1 large potato, peeled and diced

150 g / 5 ½ oz / 1 cup peas, defrosted
   if frozen

2 tbsp mint leaves, finely chopped

225 g / 8 oz / 1 cup all-butter puff pastry

1 egg, beaten

salt and pepper

Method

Heat the oil in a saucepan and fry the mince for
5 minutes or until browned. Add the onion and garlic
and fry for 5 more minutes, then stir in the stock and
potatoes and bring to the boil. Simmer for 8 minutes,
then stir in the peas and mint and season to taste with
salt and pepper.

Preheat the oven to 220°C (200°C fan) / 425F / gas 7.

Pour the lamb mixture into a baking dish and level
the top.

Roll out the pastry and lay it over the top, then press
round the edges to seal and trim away any excess pastry.
Score a few lines across the top of the pastry, being
careful not to cut all the way through.

Brush the top of the pie with egg, then bake it for
30 minutes or until the crust is golden brown and
cooked through.

Chicken pie

Serves: 4

Preparation time: 45 minutes

Cooking time: 30 minutes

Ingredients

2 tbsp butter

1 onion, chopped

1 large carrot, peeled and chopped

1 tbsp plain (all purpose) flour

500 ml / 18 fl. oz / 2 cups milk

3 cooked chicken breasts, cubed

75 g / 2 ½ oz / ½ cup peas,
   defrosted if frozen

75 g / 2 ½ oz / 1 cup button
   mushrooms, quartered

salt and pepper

For the pastry

200 g / 7 oz / 1 cup butter,
   cubed and chilled

400 g / 14 oz / 2 ⅔ cups plain
   (all purpose) flour

2 tbsp milk

Method

First make the pastry. Rub the butter into the flour until the mixture resembles fine breadcrumbs. Stir in just enough cold water to bring the pastry together into a pliable dough, then chill for 30 minutes.

Meanwhile, heat the butter in a saucepan and fry the onion and carrot for 5 minutes without colouring. Sprinkle in the flour and stir well, then stir in the milk and bubble until it thickens. Add the chicken, peas and mushrooms to the pan and heat through, then season to taste with salt and white pepper.

Preheat the oven to 200°C (180°C fan) / 400F / gas 6.

Roll out half the pastry on a lightly floured surface and use it to line a pie dish. Spoon in the filling and level the top, then brush round the rim with water.
Roll out the rest of the pastry and lay it over the top. Trim away any excess, then crimp round the edge with your thumb and forefinger.

Use the pastry trimmings to decorate the top, then brush it with milk.

Bake the pie for 30 minutes or until the pastry is cooked through underneath and golden brown on top.

Meat and Fish Pies

Salmon and potato deep dish pie

Serves: 8

Prep time: 45 minutes

Cooking time: 45 minutes

Ingredients

450 g / 1 lb / 2 ½ cups potatoes, peeled and sliced

1 clove of garlic, crushed

300 ml / 10 ½ fl. oz / 1 ¼ cups double (heavy) cream

300 g / 10 ½ oz / 2 cups salmon fillet, skinned and chopped

450 g / 1 lb / 2 cups all-butter puff pastry

1 egg, beaten

salt and pepper

Method

Preheat the oven to 200°C (180°C fan) / 400F / gas 6.

Parboil the potatoes in salted water for 10 minutes, then drain well. Toss the potatoes with the garlic and cream and season well with salt and pepper, then leave to cool to room temperature.

Roll out half the pastry on a floured surface and use it to line a deep 23 cm (9 in) spring-form cake tin. Arrange the salmon in the bottom and top with the sliced potatoes and cream.

Roll out the rest of the pastry and lay it over the top then crimp the edges to seal. Trim away any excess pastry and make a hole in the top for the steam to escape, then brush the top with beaten egg.

Bake the pie in the oven for 45 minutes or until the pastry is cooked through underneath and golden brown on top.

Serve hot or at room temperature.

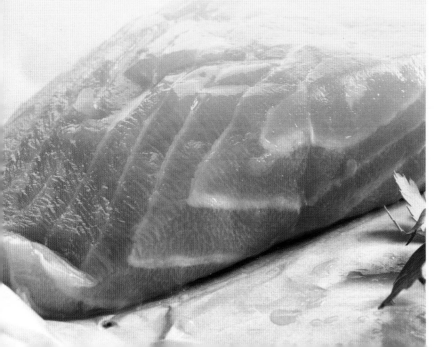

Fish and vegetable potato-topped pie

Serves: 4

Preparation time: 30 minutes

Cooking time: 30 minutes

Ingredients

450 g / 1 lb / 2 ½ cups floury potatoes, peeled and cubed

500 ml / 17 ½ fl. oz / 2 cups milk

1 bay leaf

400 g / 14 oz smoked haddock fillet

4 tbsp butter

2 tbsp plain (all purpose) flour

1 carrot, coarsely grated

1 courgette (zucchini), coarsely grated

1 yellow pepper, very thinly sliced

75 g / 2 ½ oz / ¾ cup Cheddar, grated

salt and pepper

Method

Preheat the oven to 200°C (180°C fan) / 400F / gas 6.

Cook the potatoes in boiling salted water for 12 minutes or until tender then drain well.

Meanwhile, put the milk and bay leaf in a small saucepan and bring to a simmer. Lay the haddock in a snugly fitting dish and pour the hot milk over the top. Cover the dish with cling film and leave to stand for 10 minutes.

Heat half of the butter in a small saucepan and stir in the flour. Reserve 2 tbsp of the haddock milk for the potatoes and strain the rest into the butter and flour mixture, stirring constantly. Cook until the sauce is thick and smooth.

Remove any skin and bones from the haddock, then flake the flesh into the white sauce with the vegetables. Season to taste with salt and black pepper and pour the mixture into a baking dish.

Mash the potatoes with the reserved milk and remaining butter and spoon it on top of the haddock. Sprinkle with cheese, then bake for 30 minutes or until the topping is golden brown.

Game pie

Serves: **8**

Preparation time: **30 minutes**

Cooking time: **1 hour**

Ingredients

200 g / 7 oz / 1 ⅓ cups minced pork

200 g / 7 oz / 1 ⅓ cups boneless
   rabbit, finely chopped

200 g / 7 oz / 1 ⅓ cups boneless
   venison, finely chopped

100 g / 3 ½ oz / ⅔ cup back bacon,
   finely chopped

1 onion, finely grated

½ tsp freshly grated nutmeg

salt and pepper

For the pastry:

50 g / 1 ¾ oz / ¼ cup butter

200 g / 7 oz / 1 ⅓ cups plain
   (all purpose) flour

50 g / 1 ¾ oz / ⅓ cup strong white
   bread flour

50 g / 1 ¾ oz / ¼ cup lard

1 egg, beaten

Method

First make the pastry. Rub the butter into the two flours with a teaspoon of salt until the mixture resembles fine breadcrumbs. Put the lard in a saucepan with 100 ml / 3 fl. oz / ½ cup water and bring to the boil, then stir it into the flour.

Turn the dough out onto a lightly floured work surface and knead for 1 minute or until smooth. Reserve a third of the dough for making the lid, then roll the rest out into a large rectangle.

Use the pastry to line a baking tin, allowing the edges to overhang a little.

Mix the mince, rabbit, venison, bacon, onion and nutmeg together, seasoning liberally with sea salt and white pepper. Pack the mixture into the pastry case. Roll out the reserved pastry into a rectangle large enough to cover the surface of the pie.

Brush the overhanging edges with beaten egg then lay the pastry lid over the top and crimp the edges to seal. Trim away any excess pastry and make a 1 cm (½ in) hole in the top for the steam to escape. Chill the uncooked pie for 30 minutes to firm up the pastry.

Preheat the oven to 200°C (180°C fan) / 400F / gas 6.

Brush the pastry lid with beaten egg then bake the pie for 1 hour. Leave to cool completely before serving.

32

Chicken and vegetable pie

Serves: 4

Preparation time: **45 minutes**

Cooking time: **45 minutes**

Ingredients

2 tbsp butter

200 g / 7 oz / 1 ⅓ cups
chicken breast, cubed

1 leek, chopped

1 celery stick, chopped

2 carrots, chopped

1 tsp plain (all purpose) flour

250 ml / 9 fl. oz / 1 cup chicken stock

75 g / 2 ½ oz / ½ cup peas,
defrosted if frozen

salt and pepper

For the pastry

100 g / 3 ½ oz / ½ cup butter,
cubed and chilled

200 g / 7 oz / 1 ⅓ cups plain
(all purpose) flour, plus extra
for rolling

Method

First make the pastry. Rub the butter into the flour until the mixture resembles fine breadcrumbs. Stir in just enough cold water to bring the pastry together into a pliable dough, then chill for 30 minutes.

Preheat the oven to 200°C (180°C fan) / 400F / gas 6.

Heat the butter in a saucepan and fry the chicken, leek, celery and carrots for 5 minutes without colouring. Sprinkle in the flour and stir well, then stir in the stock and bubble until it thickens slightly. Add the peas to the pan and heat through, then season to taste with salt and pepper.

Roll out half the pastry on a lightly floured surface and use to line a round pie dish. Spoon in the filling, then brush round the rim with water. Roll out the rest of the pastry to make the lid, then trim away any excess and crimp the sides.

Bake the pie for 45 minutes or until the pastry is golden brown and cooked through underneath.

Salmon coulibiac

Serves: **8**

Preparation time: **1 hour**

Cooking time: **40 minutes**

Ingredients

700 g / 1 lb 9 oz / 4 cups skinless,
    boneless salmon fillet

2 tbsp butter

1 large onion, finely chopped

1 tsp ground coriander (cilantro)

1 tsp ground cumin

200 g / 7 oz / 1 cup basmati rice

400 ml / 14 fl. oz / 1 ⅔ cups fish stock

½ lemon, juiced and zest finely grated

2 tbsp fresh dill, finely chopped

2 tbsp flat leaf parsley, finely chopped

2 tbsp chives, chopped

6 hard-boiled eggs, peeled

salt and pepper

For the pastry

200 g / 7 oz / 1 cup butter, frozen

400 g / 14 oz / 2 ⅔ cups plain
    (all purpose) flour

Method

To make the flaky pastry, grate the frozen butter into the flour and add a pinch of salt. Stir in just enough cold water to bring the pastry together into a pliable dough, then chill for 30 minutes.

Meanwhile, bring a large pan of water to the boil, then add the salmon. Cover the pan, turn off the heat and leave to poach gently for 10 minutes. Drain well.

Heat the butter in a saucepan and fry the onion for 5 minutes without colouring. Stir in the coriander, cumin and rice and cook for 1 more minute, then pour in the stock and season with salt and pepper.

When the stock starts to boil, cover the pan and turn the heat down to its lowest setting. Cook for 10 minutes, then turn off the heat and leave to stand for 10 minutes. Leave the rice to cool completely, then stir through the lemon zest and juice and the herbs.

Preheat the oven to 200°C (180°C fan) / 400F / gas 6. Roll out three quarters of the pastry on a lightly floured surface and use it to line a large loaf tin. Spoon in half of the rice, then flake in half of the salmon. Arrange the boiled eggs in a line down the centre, then top them with the rest of the salmon. Spoon over the remaining rice and level the top.

Roll out the rest of the pastry, lay it over the top and crimp the edges to seal. Bake the coulibiac for 40 minutes, then leave it to cool for 10 minutes before serving.

Mince and herb pie

Serves: 4

Preparation time: 45 minutes

Cooking time: 30 minutes

Ingerdients

2 tbsp olive oil

1 onion, finely chopped

2 cloves of garlic, finely chopped

450 g / 1 lb / 3 cups minced beef

½ tbsp fresh thyme leaves

1 tbsp flat leaf parsley

1 tbsp chives, chopped

For the pastry

400 g / 14 oz / 2 ⅔ cups plain
    (all purpose) flour

200 g / 7 oz / ¾ cup butter,
    cubed and chilled

1 egg, beaten

Method

To make the pastry, sieve the flour into a mixing bowl then rub in the butter until the mixture resembles fine breadcrumbs. Stir in just enough cold water to bring the pastry together into a pliable dough, then chill for 30 minutes.

Heat the oil in a large frying pan and fry the onion and garlic for 5 minutes without colouring. Add the minced beef and stir-fry for 5 minutes or until it starts to brown. Leave to cool, then stir in the herbs.

Preheat the oven to 200°C (180°C fan) / 400F / gas 6.

Roll out half the pastry on a floured surface and use it to line a shallow pie tin. Spoon the mince mixture inside, then moisten the edge of the pastry with a little water.

Roll out the rest of the pastry and lay it over the top, then trim away any excess pastry and crimp around the edge. Make a hole in the top for the steam to escape before brushing with beaten egg.

Bake the pie for 30 minutes or until the pastry is cooked through underneath and golden brown on top.

Chicken, chestnut and truffle pie

Serves: 6

Preparation time: 25 minutes

Cooking time: 45 minutes

Ingredients

450 g / 1 lb / 2 ½ cups floury potatoes, peeled and cubed

100 ml / 3 ½ fl. oz / ½ cup milk

50 g / 1 ¾ oz / ¼ cup butter

2 tbsp olive oil

1 onion, finely chopped

2 cloves of garlic, crushed

450 g / 1 lb / 2 cups boneless chicken thigh, cubed

200 g / 7 oz / 1 ⅓ cups cooked chestnuts

200 ml / 7 fl. oz / ¾ cup chicken stock

½ small truffle, shaved

2 tbsp dried breadcrumbs

2 tbsp Parmesan, finely grated

salt and pepper

Method

Preheat the oven to 180°C (160°C fan) / 350F / gas 4.

Boil the potatoes in salted water for 12 minutes, or until they are tender, then drain well. Return the potatoes to the saucepan and add the milk and butter, then mash until smooth.

Heat the oil in a large frying pan and fry the onion and garlic for 5 minutes without colouring. Add the chicken and fry until it starts to brown then stir in the chestnuts, stock and truffle slices. Season with salt and pepper.

Tip the mixture into a baking dish and spoon the mash on top. Mix the breadcrumbs with the Parmesan and scatter them over the top. Bake the pie for 45 minutes.

Pork and pumpkin potato pie

Serves: 6

Preparation time: **25 minutes**

Cooking time: **45 minutes**

Ingredients

450 g / 1 lb / 2 ½ cups floury potatoes,
    peeled and cubed

100 ml / 3 ½ fl. oz / ½ cup milk

50 g / 1 ¾ oz / ¼ cup butter

2 tbsp olive oil

1 onion, finely chopped

2 cloves of garlic, crushed

450 g / 1 lb / 2 cups pork mince

400 g / 14 oz / 3 cups culinary pumpkin,
    peeled and cubed

a pinch of ground cinnamon

200 ml / 7 fl. oz / ¾ cup vegetable stock

salt and pepper

Method

Preheat the oven to 180°C (160°C fan) / 350F / gas 4.

Boil the potatoes in salted water for 12 minutes, or until they are tender, then drain well. Return the potatoes to the saucepan and add the milk and butter, then mash until smooth.

Heat the oil in a large frying pan and fry the onion and garlic for 5 minutes without colouring. Add the mince and fry until it starts to brown then stir in the pumpkin, cinnamon and stock. Season with salt and pepper.

Tip the mixture into a baking dish and spoon the mash on top. Bake the pie for 45 minutes.

Turkey and vegetable pie

Serves: 4

Preparation time: 30 minutes

Cooking time: 45 minutes

Ingredients

2 tbsp butter

1 onion, chopped

1 carrot, chopped

1 celery stick, chopped

1 tbsp plain (all purpose) flour

250 ml / 9 fl. oz / 1 cups milk

300 g / 10 ½ oz / 2 cups cooked turkey
   breast, cubed

150 ml / 5 ½ fl. oz / ⅔ cup crème fraiche

2 tbsp flat leaf parsley, finely chopped

450 g / 1 lb all-butter puff pastry

1 egg, beaten

salt and pepper

Method

Heat the butter in a saucepan and fry the onion, carrot and celery for 10 minutes without colouring. Sprinkle in the flour and stir well, then stir in the milk and bubble until it thickens. Add the turkey and crème fraiche and heat through, then season to taste with salt and white pepper. Stir in the parsley then leave to cool completely.

Preheat the oven to 200°C (180°C fan) / 400F / gas 6.

Roll out half the pastry on a lightly floured surface and use it to line a pie dish. Spoon in the filling and level the top, then brush round the rim with water. Roll out the rest of the pastry and lay it over the top then trim away any excess.

Brush the top of the pie with beaten egg then bake for 45 minutes or until the pastry is cooked through underneath and golden brown on top.

Beef and onion free-form pie

Serves: 4

Preparation time: **45 minutes**

Cooking time: **40 minutes**

Ingredients

2 tbsp olive oil

2 red onions, sliced

3 cloves of garlic, finely chopped

450 g / 1 lb / 3 cups sirloin steak, cubed

250 g / 9 oz / 1 ¼ cup all-butter puff pastry

1 egg, beaten

salt and pepper

Method

Heat the oil in a frying pan and fry the onions for 20 minutes, stirring occasionally to soften and caramelise them. Take the pan off the heat and leave to cool, then stir in the garlic and steak and season well with salt and pepper.

Preheat the oven to 220°C (200°C fan) / 425F / gas 7.

Roll out half the pastry on a floured surface into a large circle and brush round the edge with beaten egg. Pile the filling on top. Roll out the rest of the pastry into a circle a little smaller than the base. Lay it on top, then bring up the sides of the pastry and crimp to seal. Trim away any excess and use the offcuts to decorate the top.

Brush the pie with egg, then bake for 40 minutes or until the pastry is cooked through and crisp underneath.

Cheese, bacon and tomato quiche

Serves: 6

Preparation time: 1 hour

Cooking time: 40 minutes

Ingredients

225 g / 8 oz / 1 cup all-butter puff pastry

200 g / 7 oz / 1 ½ cups smoked
    bacon lardons

2 tbsp olive oil

3 large eggs, beaten

225 ml / 8 fl. oz / ¾ cup double
    (heavy) cream

2 tomatoes, cut into wedges

150 g / 5 ½ oz / 1½ cups Gruyère, grated

salt and pepper

Method

Preheat the oven to 190°C (170°C fan) / 375F / gas 5.

Roll out the pastry on a floured surface and use it to line a 23 cm (9 in) round tart tin. Prick the pastry with a fork, line with cling film and fill with baking beans or rice. Bake the case for 10 minutes, then remove the cling film and baking beans. Brush the inside with beaten egg and return to the oven for 8 minutes to crisp.

Lower the oven to 150°C (130°C fan) / 300F / gas 2.

Fry the lardons in the oil for 5 minutes or until starting to brown.

Whisk the eggs with the double cream until smoothly combined then stir in the lardons, tomatoes and half of the Gruyère. Season generously with salt and pepper.

Pour the filling into the pastry case and scatter the rest of the cheese on top. Bake for 40 minutes or until just set in the centre.

48

Vegetable Pies

Feta and mushroom turnovers

Makes: 6

Preparation time: 30 minutes

Cooking time: 18 minutes

Ingredients

2 tbsp butter

½ onion, finely chopped

150 g / 5 oz / 2 cups chestnut
    mushrooms, sliced

1 garlic clove, crushed

100 g / 3 ½ oz / 4 cups baby leaf spinach

100 g / 3 ½ oz / ½ cup feta
    cheese, crumbled

700 g / 1 ½ lb / 3 ¼ cups all-butter
    puff pastry

1 egg, beaten

salt and pepper

Method

Heat the butter in a frying pan and fry the onion for
5 minutes or until translucent. Add the mushrooms
and garlic and cook for 5 more minutes, stirring
occasionally until golden. Stir in the spinach and let it
wilt down, then tip everything into a bowl and let it cool
to room temperature.

Preheat the oven to 220°C (200°C fan) / 425F / gas 7.

Stir the feta into the mushroom mixture and season to
taste with salt and pepper.

Roll out the pastry on a lightly floured surface and cut
out 6 circles. Divide the filling between them and brush
round the edge with egg.

Fold the pastry in half and crimp around the edges.

Brush the turnovers with beaten egg and bake for
18 minutes or until golden brown and cooked through.

Spinach turnovers

Makes: 4

Preparation time: 45 minutes

Cooking time: 20 minutes

Ingredients

2 tbsp olive oil

1 onion, finely chopped

2 cloves of garlic, crushed

100 g / 3 ½ oz / 4 cups young
    spinach leaves, washed

½ tsp freshly grated nutmeg

75 g / 2 ½ oz / ¾ cup halloumi
    cheese, grated

1 tbsp mint leaves, chopped

1 tbsp fresh dill, chopped

salt and pepper

For the pastry

100 g / 3 ½ oz / ½ cup butter,
    cubed and chilled

200 g / 7 oz / 1 ⅓ cups plain
    (all purpose) flour

Method

First make the pastry. Rub the butter into the flour until the mixture resembles fine breadcrumbs. Stir in just enough cold water to bring the pastry together into a pliable dough, then chill for 30 minutes.

Meanwhile, heat the oil in a large saucepan and fry the onion and garlic for 5 minutes without colouring. Stir in the spinach until it wilts right down, then take the pan off the heat and stir in the nutmeg, halloumi and herbs. Season to taste with salt and pepper.

Preheat the oven to 200°C (180°C fan) / 400F / gas 6.

Roll out the pastry on a lightly floured surface and cut it into 4 squares. Brush round the edge of the squares with water, then divide the spinach mixture between them.

Fold each pastry square in half to form a triangle and completely encase the filling. Crimp around the edges with a fork to seal and prick a few holes in the top of each one.

Bake the turnovers for 20 minutes or until the pastry is cooked through and crisp underneath.

Aubergine turnover

Serves: 2

Preparation time: 30 minutes

Cooking time: 30 minutes

Ingredients

1 large aubergine (eggplant), sliced
  lengthways

3 tbsp olive oil

4 tbsp sun-dried tomato pesto

1 mozzarella ball, sliced

225 g / 8 oz / 1 cup all-butter puff pastry

1 egg, beaten

salt and pepper

Method

Heat a griddle pan until smoking hot. Brush the aubergine slices with oil and season with salt and pepper, then griddle them for 4 minutes on each side or until nicely marked. Leave to cool.

Preheat the oven to 220°C (200°C fan) / 425F / gas 7.

Roll out the pastry into a large square. Layer up the aubergine, pesto, and mozzarella on one side of the square, then brush round the edge with beaten egg.

Fold over the pastry and crimp round the edge to seal, then cut away any excess pastry. Decorate the top of the turnover with the offcuts, then brush the top with beaten egg.

Bake the turnover for 30 minutes or until the pastry is cooked through underneath and golden brown on top.

Vegetable pot pies

Makes: 4

Preparation time: 45 minutes

Cooking time: 20 minutes

Ingredients

2 tbsp olive oil

1 onion, chopped

1 yellow pepper, diced

1 courgette (zucchini), diced

½ head of broccoli, diced

2 cloves of garlic, crushed

100 ml / 3 ½ fl. oz / ½ cup dry
   white wine

salt and pepper

For the pastry

100 g / 3 ½ oz / ½ cup butter,
   cubed and chilled

200 g / 7 oz / 1 ⅓ cups plain
   (all purpose) flour

1 tsp sesame seeds

Method

First make the pastry. Rub the butter into the flour until the mixture resembles fine breadcrumbs. Stir in just enough cold water to bring the pastry together into a pliable dough, then chill for 30 minutes.

Meanwhile, heat the oil in a frying pan fry the onion and peppers for 5 minutes to soften. Add the courgette, broccoli and garlic and stir-fry for 5 more minutes, then pour in the wine. Bubble for 2 minutes, then season well with salt and pepper.

Preheat the oven to 200°C (180°C fan) / 400F / gas 6.

Roll out the pastry on a lightly floured surface and cut out 4 circles. Divide the filling between four individual pie dishes and brush the rims with water. Top each pie with a pastry lid and press around the edges firmly to seal.

Sprinkle the tops with sesame seeds, then bake for 20 minutes or until the pastry is golden brown.

Mushroom and leek filo pies

Makes: 4

Preparation time: 30 minutes

Cooking time: 15 minutes

Ingredients

2 tbsp olive oil

1 large leek, chopped

2 cloves of garlic, crushed

250 g / 9 oz / 3 cups button
 mushrooms, quartered

100 g / 3 ½ oz / ⅔ cup peas, defrosted
 if frozen

100 ml / 3 ½ fl. oz / ½ cup dry white wine

8 sheets filo pastry

50 g / 1 ¾ oz / ¼ cup butter, melted

salt and pepper

Method

Heat the oil in a frying pan and fry the leek and garlic for 5 minutes without colouring. Add the mushrooms to the pan and season with salt and pepper, then cook for 10 minutes, stirring occasionally. Add the peas and wine and bubble until reduced by half. Season to taste with salt and pepper.

Preheat the oven to 200°C (180°C fan) / 400F / gas 6.

Divide the filling between 4 individual pie dishes. Brush the filo with melted butter, then scrunch up the sheets and lay them on top.

Bake the pies for 15 minutes or until the pastry is crisp and golden brown.

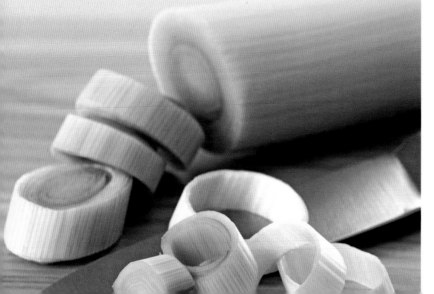

Cheese and potato pie

Serves: 6

Preparation time: 30 minutes

Cooking time: 45 minutes

Ingredients

450 g / 1 lb / 2 ½ cups potatoes, peeled
   and sliced

1 clove of garlic, crushed

300 ml / 10 ½ fl. oz / 1 ¼ cups double
   (heavy) cream

2 tbsp thyme leaves

100 g / 3 ½ oz / 1 cup Gruyère
   cheese, grated

450 g / 1 lb / 2 cups all-butter
   puff pastry

1 egg, beaten

salt and pepper

Method

Preheat the oven to 200°C (180°C fan) / 400F / gas 6.

Par-boil the potatoes in salted water for 10 minutes, then drain well. Toss the potatoes with the garlic, cream, thyme and Gruyère and season well with salt and pepper, then leave to cool to room temperature.

Roll out half the pastry on a floured surface and use it to line a pie dish. Pack the potatoes in tightly and pour over any cream left in the bowl.

Roll out the rest of the pastry and lay it over the top then crimp the edges to seal. Trim away any excess pastry, then brush the top with beaten egg.

Bake the pie in the oven for 45 minutes or until the pastry is cooked through underneath and golden brown on top.

Vegetarian mince and bean pie

Serves: 6

Preparation time: 25 minutes

Cooking time: 3 hours

Ingredients

2 tbsp olive oil

1 onion, sliced

1 red pepper, diced

2 cloves of garlic, crushed

450 g / 1 lb / 2 cups vegetarian mince

400 g / 14 oz / 1 ¾ cups canned
    tomatoes, chopped

200 ml / 7 fl. oz / ¾ cup vegetable stock

400 g / 14 oz / 1 ¾ cups canned haricot
    beans, drained

400 g / 14 oz / 2 cups Maris Piper
    potatoes, sliced

50 g / 1 ¾ oz / ¼ cup butter, cubed

Method

Preheat the oven to 160°C (140°C fan) / 325F / gas 3.

Heat the oil in a large frying pan and fry the onion,
pepper and garlic for 10 minutes, stirring occasionally.
Add the mince and fry until it starts to brown, then stir
in the tomatoes, stock and beans.

Scrape the mixture into a baking dish and arrange the
potato slices in top. Cover the dish with foil and bake
for 2 hours.

Remove the foil and dot the surface of the hot pot with
butter then bake for 1 more hour.

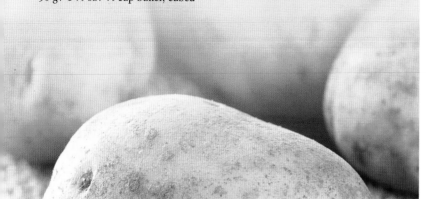

Individual Pies

Steak and kidney pie

Makes: 4

Preparation time: 2 hours 40 minutes

Cooking time: 45 minutes

Ingredients

4 tbsp olive oil

1 kg / 2 lb 3 oz / 5 cups braising
   steak, cubed

4 lamb's kidneys, trimmed and cubed

1 onion, finely chopped

3 cloves of garlic, finely chopped

2 bay leaves

600 ml / 1 pint / 2 ½ cups good quality
   beef stock

250 g / 9 oz / 3 cups mushrooms,
   quartered

450 g / 1 lb / 2 cups all-butter
   puff pastry

1 egg, beaten

salt and pepper

Method

Heat the oil in an ovenproof saucepan and sear the steak and kidney in batches until well browned. Remove the meat from the pan, add the onions, garlic, and bay leaves and cook for 5 minutes.

Pour in the stock and return the beef, then simmer for 2 hours. 30 minutes before the end of the cooking time, season to taste with salt and pepper and stir in the mushrooms. Leave to cool completely.

Preheat the oven to 220°C (200°C fan) / 425F / gas 7.

Roll out two thirds of the pastry and use it to line 4 individual pie dishes. Ladle the pie filling into the pastry cases and brush round the edges with beaten egg.

Roll out the rest of the pastry and lay it over the tops of the pies, then trim away the excess pastry. Scallop the edges and decorate the tops with shapes cut from the offcuts, then brush with beaten egg and make a hole for the steam to escape.

Bake the pie for 45 minutes or until the pastry is golden brown and cooked through.

Lamb and rosemary pot pies

Makes: 4

Preparation time: 45 minutes

Cooking time: 20 minutes

Ingredients

2 tbsp olive oil

2 lamb leg steaks, sliced

1 onion, sliced

1 red pepper, sliced

1 green pepper, sliced

2 cloves of garlic, crushed

1 tsp dried rosemary

2 tbsp redcurrant jelly

100 ml / 3 ½ fl. oz / ½ cup dry
   white wine

For the pastry

100 g / 3 ½ oz / ½ cup butter,
   cubed and chilled

200 g / 7 oz / 1 ⅓ cups plain
   (all purpose) flour

1 tsp dried rosemary

Method

First make the pastry. Rub the butter into the flour until the mixture resembles fine breadcrumbs. Stir in just enough cold water to bring the pastry together into a pliable dough, then chill for 30 minutes.

Meanwhile, heat the oil in a frying pan and stir-fry the lamb for 2 minutes. Add the onion and peppers and fry for 5 minutes, then stir in the garlic and rosemary. Cook for 1 more minute, then stir in the redcurrant jelly and pour in the wine. Bubble gently for 2 minutes, then take the pan off the heat.

Preheat the oven to 200°C (180°C fan) / 400F / gas 6.

Roll out the pastry on a lightly floured surface and cut out 4 circles. Divide the filling between 4 individual pie dishes and brush the rims with water. Top each pie with a pastry lid and press around the edges firmly to seal.

Make five slashes across the top of each pie and sprinkle with rosemary. Bake the pies for 20 minutes or until the pastry is golden brown.

Salmon pot pies

Makes: 4

Preparation time: 25 minutes

Cooking time: 25 minutes

Ingredients

2 tbsp butter

1 tsp plain (all purpose) flour

250 ml / 9 fl. oz / 1 cup milk

200 g / 7 oz / 1 ⅓ cups salmon fillet, cubed

2 tbsp chives, chopped

250 g / 9 oz / 1 ¼ cups all-butter puff pastry

1 egg, beaten

salt and pepper

Method

Preheat the oven to 200°C (180°C fan) / 400F / gas 6.

Heat the butter in a saucepan then stir in the flour and cook for 30 seconds. Gradually incorporate the milk, stirring all the time, then bring to a gentle simmer.

Stir in the salmon and chives then season with salt and pepper and divide the mixture between four mini casserole dishes.

Roll out the pastry on a lightly floured surface and cut out four circles. Top each dish with a pastry lid and press around the edges to seal.

Brush the tops with beaten egg then bake for 25 minutes or until the pastry is golden brown and puffy.

Confit duck pies

Makes: 4

Preparation time: 45 minutes

Cooking time: 35 minutes

Ingredients

1 large potato, peeled and diced

2 confit duck legs

1 onion, finely chopped

2 cloves of garlic, finely chopped

450 g / 1 lb / 2 cups all-butter
    puff pastry

1 egg, beaten

Method

Preheat the oven to 200°C (180°C fan) / 400F / gas 6.

Parboil the potatoes in salted water for 5 minutes, then drain well.

Meanwhile, fry the confit duck legs for 5 minutes on each side, then remove them from the pan. Fry the onion and garlic in the fat from the duck for 5 minutes without colouring. Shred the duck and discard the bones, then toss the meat with the potatoes and onions. Leave to cool a little.

Roll out two thirds of the pastry on a lightly floured surface and use it to line 4 individual pie dishes. Spoon the duck mixture into the pastry cases.

Roll out the rest of the pastry and make the lids, then crimp around the outsides with a fork.

Brush the tops with beaten egg then bake for 35 minutes or until the pastry is cooked through underneath and golden brown on top.

Prawn and potato pot pies

Makes: 4

Preparation time: 45 minutes

Cooking time: 30 minutes

Ingredients

2 tbsp butter

1 onion, chopped

2 potatoes, peeled and diced

1 tsp plain (all purpose) flour

250 ml / 9 fl. oz / 1 cup milk

200 g / 7 oz / 1 ⅓ cups prawns
   (shrimp) peeled

2 tbsp flat leaf parsley, finely chopped

For the pastry

100 g / 3 ½ oz / ½ cup butter,
   cubed and chilled

200 g / 7 oz / 1 ⅓ cups plain
   (all purpose) flour

1 large egg, beaten

Method

First make the pastry. Rub the butter into the flour until the mixture resembles fine breadcrumbs. Stir in just enough cold water to bring the pastry together into a pliable dough, then chill for 30 minutes.

Preheat the oven to 200°C (180°C fan) / 400F / gas 6.

Heat the butter in a saucepan and fry the onion and potato for 5 minutes without colouring.

Sprinkle in the flour and stir well, then stir in the milk and bubble until it thickens slightly.

Season to taste with salt and white pepper, then stir in the prawns and parsley.

Roll out the pastry on a lightly floured surface and cut out 4 circles. Divide the filling between 4 individual pie dishes and brush the rims with water. Top each pie with a pastry lid and press around the edges firmly to seal.

Brush the tops with beaten egg, then bake the pies for 30 minutes or until the pastry is golden brown.

Chicken and carrot pot pies

Makes: 4

Preparation time: 45 minutes

Cooking time: 30 minutes

Ingredients

2 tbsp butter

1 onion, chopped

2 carrots, chopped

1 tsp plain (all purpose) flour

250 ml / 9 fl. oz / 1 cup milk

200 g / 7 oz / 1 ⅓ cups
  cooked chicken
  breast, cubed

½ tbsp fresh thyme leaves

salt and pepper

For the pastry

100 g / 3 ½ oz / ½ cup butter, frozen

200 g / 7 oz / 1 ⅓ cups plain
  (all purpose) flour

1 egg, beaten

thyme sprigs to garnish

Method

To make the flaky pastry, grate the frozen butter into the flour and add a pinch of salt. Stir in just enough cold water to bring the pastry together into a pliable dough, then chill for 30 minutes.

Preheat the oven to 200°C (180°C fan) / 400F / gas 6.

Heat the butter in a saucepan and fry the onion and carrot for 5 minutes without colouring. Sprinkle in the flour and stir well, then stir in the milk and bubble until it thickens slightly. Add the chicken and heat through, then season to taste with salt and white pepper.

Roll out the pastry on a lightly floured surface and cut out 4 circles. Divide the filling between 4 individual pie dishes and brush the rims with water. Top each pie with a pastry lid and crimp the edges to seal. Brush the tops with beaten egg.

Bake the pies for 30 minutes or until the pastry is golden brown. Garnish with thyme sprigs before serving.

Individual wild mushroom pies

Makes: 4

Preparation time: 45 minutes

Cooking time: 30 minutes

Ingredients

2 tbsp butter

4 shallots, finely chopped

2 cloves of garlic, crushed

250 g / 9 oz / 3 ⅓ cups wild
   mushrooms, cleaned

100 ml / 3 ½ fl. oz / ½ cup dry white wine

100 ml / 3 ½ fl. oz / ½ cup double
   (heavy) cream

2 tbsp flat leaf parsley, chopped

salt and pepper

For the pastry

200 g / 7 oz / 1 cup butter, cubed
   and chilled

400 g / 14 oz / 2 ⅔ cups plain (all
   purpose) flour

1 egg, beaten

Method

First make the pastry. Rub the butter into the flour until the mixture resembles fine breadcrumbs. Stir in just enough cold water to bring the pastry together into a pliable dough, then chill for 30 minutes.

Meanwhile, heat the butter in a frying pan and fry the shallots and garlic for 5 minutes without colouring. Add the mushrooms to the pan and season with salt and pepper, then cook for 10 minutes, stirring occasionally. Pour in the white wine and bubble until it has reduced by half. Stir in the cream and parsley, then taste for seasoning. Leave to cool completely.

Preheat the oven to 200°C (180°C fan) / 400F / gas 6.

Roll out two thirds of the pastry on a lightly floured surface and use it to line 4 individual pie dishes. Divide the filling between them and brush the rims with water.

Roll out the rest of the pastry and cut out 4 lids, making a hole in the centres so the steam can escape. Lay the lids on top of the pies, then fold the edges over the top and crimp to seal.

Brush the pies with beaten egg, then bake for 30 minutes or until the pastry is golden brown and cooked through underneath.

Lamb and apple potato-topped pies

Serves: 6

Preparation time: 15 minutes

Cooking time: 3 hours 15 minutes

Ingredients

300 ml / 10 ½ fl. oz / 1 ¼ cups
   lamb stock
600 g/ 1 lb 5 oz / 3 cups lamb
   shoulder, sliced
3 onions, sliced
1 Bramley apple, peeled, cored,
   and diced
salt and pepper

For the topping

450 g / 1 lb / 2 ½ cups floury
   potatoes, peeled and cubed
100 ml / 3 ½ fl. oz / ½ cup milk
50 g / 1 ¾ oz / ¼ cup butter
1 eating apple, cored and diced

Method

Preheat the oven to 150°C (130°C fan) / 300F / gas 2 and bring the stock to boiling.

Mix the lamb, onions, and Bramley apple together in a cast iron casserole dish and season well with salt and pepper. Pour the hot stock over the mixture. Then cover the dish and transfer to the oven for 3 hours.

Meanwhile, boil the potatoes in salted water for 12 minutes, or until they are tender, then drain well. Return the potatoes to the saucepan and add the milk and butter, then mash until smooth.

Season the lamb mixture to taste, then divide between 6 individual gratin dishes. Increase the oven temperature to 200°C (180°C fan) / 400F / gas 6.

Spoon the mash on top of the lamb and scatter the tops with diced apple. Transfer the gratin dishes to the oven and bake for 15 minutes or until the apple pieces are just starting to colour at the edges.

Individual cottage pies

Makes: 4

Preparation time: 1 hour 15 minutes

Cooking time: 25 minutes

Ingredients

2 tbsp olive oil

1 small onion, finely chopped

2 cloves of garlic, crushed

200 g / 7 oz / 1 cup minced beef

200 g / 7 oz / 1 cup canned
   tomatoes, chopped

200 ml / 7 fl. oz / ¾ cups beef stock

For the pastry

100 g / 3 ½ oz / ½ cup butter, cubed

200 g / 7 oz / 1 ⅓ cups plain
   (all purpose) flour

For the topping

450 g / 1 lb floury potatoes,
   peeled and cubed

100 ml / 3 ½ fl. oz / ½ cup milk

50 g / 1 ¾ oz / ¼ cup butter

50 g / 1 ¾ oz / ½ cup Cheddar,
   grated

Method

Heat the oil in a saucepan and fry the onion and garlic for 3 minutes. Add the mince and fry for 2 minutes then add the tomatoes and stock and bring to a gentle simmer. Cook for 1 hour, stirring occasionally, until the mince is tender.

Meanwhile, make the pastry. Rub the butter into the flour and add just enough cold water to bind. Chill for 30 minutes, then roll out on a floured surface.

Preheat the oven to 200°C (180°C fan) / 400F / gas 6.

Use the pastry to line 4 individual tart cases and prick the bases with a fork. Line the pastry with cling film and fill with baking beans, then bake for 10 minutes.

Meanwhile, cook the potatoes in salted water for 10 minutes, or until they are tender, then drain well. Return the potatoes to the saucepan and add the milk and butter. Mash the potatoes until smooth.

Remove the cling film and beans from the pastry cases and fill them with the mince mixture.

Top with the mashed potato, sprinkle with cheese, and bake for 15 minutes.

Chicken, pea and leek pot pies

Makes: 4

Preparation time: 25 minutes

Cooking time: 20 minutes

Ingredients

2 tbsp butter

2 leeks, chopped

2 tsp plain (all purpose) flour

250 ml / 9 fl. oz / 1 cup milk

200 g / 7 oz / 1 ⅓ cups cooked chicken
breast, cubed

150 g / 5 ½ oz / 1 cup peas, defrosted
if frozen

½ tbsp fresh thyme leaves

225 g / 8 oz / 1 cup all-butter puff pastry

salt and pepper

Method

Preheat the oven to 200°C (180°C fan) / 400F / gas 6.

Heat the butter in a saucepan and fry the leeks for
5 minutes without colouring. Sprinkle in the flour
and stir well, then stir in the milk and bubble until
it thickens slightly. Add the chicken and peas and
heat through, then season to taste with salt and
white pepper.

Roll out the pastry on a lightly floured surface and cut
out 4 circles. Divide the filling between 4 individual pie
dishes and brush the rims with water. Top each pie with
a pastry lid and crimp the edges to seal. Brush the tops
with beaten egg.

Bake the pies for 20 minutes or until the pastry is
golden brown.

Sweet Pies

Sweet Pies

Biscuit crust custard tarts

Makes: 8

Preparation time: 15 minutes

Cooking time: 20 minutes

Ingredients

50 g / 1 ¾ oz / ¼ cup butter
200 g / 7 oz / 1 ⅓ cups shortcrust
    biscuits, crushed
2 large egg yolks, beaten
50 g / 1 ¾ oz / ¼ cup caster
    (superfine) sugar
2 tsp cornflour (cornstarch)
225 ml / 8 fl. oz / ¾ cup whole milk
½ lemon, zest finely grated
½ tsp ground cinnamon
sugar nibs and mini sugar shapes
    to decorate

Method

Preheat the oven to 160°C (140°C fan) / 325F / gas 3.

Melt the butter, then stir in the biscuit crumbs. Divide it between 8 tartlet tins and firm the base and sides with your fingers.

Mix the rest of the ingredients together in a jug, then pour it into the tart cases.

Transfer the tins to the oven and bake for 20 minutes or until the custard is just set in the centre.

Decorate the tarts with sugar nibs and sugar shapes.

90

Walnut frangipane tarts

Makes: 4

Preparation time: 45 minutes

Cooking time: 25 minutes

Ingredients

75 g / 2 ½ oz / ¾ cup ground walnuts

75 g / 2 ½ oz / ⅓ cup butter, softened

75 g / 2 ½ oz / ⅓ cup caster
(superfine) sugar

1 large egg

1 tbsp plain (all purpose) flour

300 ml / 10 ½ fl. oz / 1 ¼ cups double
(heavy) cream

For the pastry

225 g / 8 oz / 1 ½ cups plain
(all purpose) flour

110 g / 4 oz / ½ cup butter, cubed
and chilled

Method

Sieve the flour into a mixing bowl, then rub in the butter until the mixture resembles fine breadcrumbs. Stir in just enough cold water to bring the pastry together into a pliable dough, then chill for 30 minutes.

Preheat the oven to 200°C (180°C fan) / 400F / gas 6.

Roll out the pastry on a floured surface and use it to line 4 individual tart cases.

Whisk together the walnuts, butter, sugar, eggs and flour until smoothly whipped, then spoon the mixture into the pastry cases.

Bake the tarts for 25 minutes or until golden brown on top and cooked through underneath. Leave to cool completely.

Whip the cream until it holds its shape, then spoon it into a piping bag fitted with a large plain nozzle. Pipe some cream onto each tart and serve immediately.

Lemon meringue pie

Serves: 8

Preparation time: 45 minutes

Cooking time: 30 minutes

Ingredients

2 tsp cornflour (cornstarch)

4 lemons, juiced and zest finely grated

4 large eggs, beaten

225 g / 8 oz / 1 cup butter

175 g / 6 oz / ¾ cup caster
(superfine) sugar

For the pastry

100 g / 3 ½ oz / ½ cup butter, cubed

200 g / 7 oz / 1 ⅓ cups plain
(all purpose) flour

2 tbsp caster (superfine) sugar

For the meringue

4 large egg whites

100g / 3 ½ oz / ½ cup caster
(superfine) sugar

Method

Preheat the oven to 200°C (180°C fan) / 400F / gas 6.

Rub the butter into the flour and sugar then add just enough cold water to bind. Chill for 30 minutes, then roll out on a floured surface. Use the pastry to line a 24 cm (9 in) loose-bottomed tart tin and prick it with a fork.

Line the pastry with cling film and fill with baking beans or rice, then bake for 10 minutes. Remove the cling film and beans and cook for another 8 minutes to crisp.

Meanwhile, dissolve the cornflour in the lemon juice and put it in a saucepan with the rest of the ingredients. Stir constantly over a medium heat to melt the butter and dissolve the sugar. Bring to a gentle simmer then pour it into the pastry case.

Whisk the egg whites until stiff, then gradually add the sugar and whisk until the mixture is thick and shiny. Spoon the meringue on top of the lemon mixture and make peaks with the spoon. Bake for 10 minutes or until golden brown.

Plum pie

Serves: 6

Preparation time: 15 minutes

Cooking time: 35–40 minutes

Ingredients

450 g / 1 lb / 2 cups all-butter puff pastry

450 g / 1 lb / 2 ½ cups plums, stoned
   and chopped

3 tbsp caster (superfine) sugar

2 tsp cornflour (cornstarch)

1 egg, beaten

Method

Preheat the oven to 200°C (180°C fan) / 400F / gas 6.

Roll out half the pastry on a floured surface and use it to line a pie dish.

Toss the plums with the sugar and cornflour and pack them into the pastry case.

Roll out the other half of the pastry. Brush the rim of the bottom crust with beaten egg, then lay the pie lid on top and press firmly around the edges to seal.

Trim away any excess pastry and use the scraps to decorate the top.

Brush the top of the pie with beaten egg and bake for 35–40 minutes or until the pastry is golden brown and cooked through underneath.

Cherry pies

Makes: 6

Preparation time: 45 minutes

Cooking time: 30 minute

Ingredients

400 g / 14 oz / 2 ⅔ cups plain (all purpose)
    flour
200 g / 7 oz / ¾ cup butter, cubed
    and chilled
400 g / 14 oz / 2 ⅔ cups cherries, stoned
4 tbsp caster (superfine) sugar
1 tsp cornflour (cornstarch)
1 egg, beaten

Method

Sieve the flour into a mixing bowl, then rub in the butter until the mixture resembles fine breadcrumbs. Stir in just enough cold water to bring the pastry together into a pliable dough. Wrap the dough in cling film and chill in the fridge for 30 minutes.

Meanwhile, preheat the oven to 200°C (180°C fan) / 400F / gas 6.

Roll out two thirds of the pastry on a floured surface and cut out 6 circles, then use them to line 6 deep pie tins.

Toss the cherries with the sugar and cornflour and divide the mixture between the 6 pastry cases. Roll out the rest of the pastry and cut out 6 circles for the lids. Brush the rim of the pastry cases with egg before laying the lids on top, then press down firmly around the outside to seal.

Trim away any excess pastry and crimp around the edges with your thumb and forefinger.

Brush the top of the pies with beaten egg, then bake in the oven for 30 minutes or until the tops are golden and the pastry underneath has cooked all the way through.

Apple and hazelnut pie

Serves: 8

Preparation time: 45 minutes

Cooking time: 45 minutes

Ingredients

55 g / 2 oz / ½ cup ground hazelnuts (cobnuts)

55 g / 2 oz / ¼ cup caster (superfine) sugar

55 g / 2 oz / ¼ cup butter, softened

1 large egg

1 tsp almond essence

1 large Bramley apple, peeled, cored and thinly sliced

For the pastry

200 g / 7 oz / 1 cup butter, cubed and chilled

400 g / 14 oz / 2 ⅔ cups plain (all purpose) flour

1 egg, beaten

2 tbsp hazelnuts (cobnuts), chopped

Method

Preheat the oven to 200°C (180°C fan) / 400F / gas 6.

To make the pastry, rub the butter into the flour, then add just enough cold water to bind the mixture together into a pliable dough. Roll out half of the pastry on a floured surface and use it to line a shallow pie dish.

Combine the ground hazelnuts, sugar, butter, egg and almond essence in a bowl and whisk together for 2 minutes or until smooth. Fold in the apple slices, then pack the mixture into the pastry case.

Roll out the rest of the pastry and lay it over the top. Trim away any excess, then roll the edges in and crimp to seal. Make a hole in the centre for the steam to escape.

Brush the top of the pie with beaten egg and sprinkle with hazelnuts, then bake for 45 minutes or until a skewer inserted in the centre comes out clean.

Blueberry pies

Makes: 6

Preparation time: 1 hour

Cooking time: 25 minutes

Ingredients

400 g / 14 oz / 2 ⅔ cups plain
  (all purpose) flour
200 g / 7 oz / ¾ cup butter, cubed
  and chilled
400 g / 14 oz / 2 ⅔ cups blueberries
4 tbsp caster (superfine) sugar
½ tsp cornflour (cornstarch)
1 egg, beaten

Method

Sieve the flour into a mixing bowl, then rub in the butter until the mixture resembles fine breadcrumbs. Stir in just enough cold water to bring the pastry together into a pliable dough. Wrap the dough in cling film and chill in the fridge for 30 minutes.

Meanwhile, preheat the oven to 200°C (180°C fan) / 400F / gas 6.

Roll out half the pastry on a floured surface and cut out 6 circles, then use them to line 6 tartlet tins. Toss the blueberries with the sugar and cornflour and divide between the 6 pastry cases.

Roll out the rest of the pastry and cut out 6 circles for the lids. Brush the rim of the pastry cases with egg before laying the lid on top, then press down firmly around the outside to seal.

Trim away any excess pastry and roll it out again. Cut the pastry into long strips and attach them to the top of the pies in a lattice pattern with a little beaten egg.

Brush the top of the pies with more beaten egg then bake in the oven for 25 minutes, or until the tops are golden and the pastry underneath has cooked all the way through.

Apple and sultana lattice pie

Serves: 8

Preparation time: 50 minutes

Cooking time: 45 minutes

Ingredients

1 kg / 2 lb 3 oz / 5 cups Bramley apples

125 g / 4 ½ oz / ½ cup caster
   (superfine) sugar

2 tbsp plain (all purpose) flour

1 tsp ground cinnamon

75 g / 2 ½ oz / ⅓ cup sultanas

For the pastry

200 g / 7 oz / 1 ⅓ cups plain
   (all purpose) flour

200 g / 7 oz / 1 ⅓ cups
   wholemeal flour

2 tbsp light brown sugar

200 g / 7 oz / ¾ cup butter, cubed

icing (confectioners')
   sugar for dusting

Method

First make the pastry. Mix the plain flour, wholemeal flour, and sugar together, then rub in the butter until it resembles fine breadcrumbs. Add just enough cold water to bring the mixture together into a pliable dough, then wrap in cling film and chill for 30 minutes.

Preheat the oven to 190°C (170°C fan) / 375F / gas 5.

Peel, core, and quarter the apples, then slice them thinly and blot away any excess moisture with kitchen paper.

Mix the sugar, flour, cinnamon and sultanas together in a bowl, then toss with the apples.

Set a third of the pastry aside, then roll out the rest on a lightly floured surface and use it to line a deep pie tin. Pack the apple mixture in tightly.

Roll out the reserved pastry, then roll a lattice cutter over the top. Gently ease the pastry apart to show the holes, then transfer it to the top of the pie and secure with a dab of water. Trim away any excess pastry.

Bake the pie for 45 minutes or until the apples are tender in the centre and the pastry is crisp underneath.

Blueberry lattice tartlets

Makes: 4

Preparation time: **1 hour**

Cooking time: **25 minutes**

Ingredients

225 g / 8 oz / 1 ½ cups plain
   (all purpose) flour
110 g / 4 oz / ½ cup butter, cubed
   and chilled
150 g / 5 ½ oz / 1 cup blueberries
225 g / 8 oz / 1 cup blueberry jam (jelly)
1 egg, beaten

Method

Preheat the oven to 200°C (180°C fan) / 400F / gas 6.

Sieve the flour into a mixing bowl, then rub in the butter until the mixture resembles fine breadcrumbs. Stir in just enough cold water to bring the pastry together into a pliable dough. Chill for 30 minutes.

Roll out the pastry on a floured surface and cut out 4 circles then use them to line 4 tartlet tins. Re-roll the trimmings and cut the sheet into 1 cm (½ in) strips.

Mix the blueberries with the jam and spoon it into the pastry cases. Lay the pastry strips over the top in a lattice pattern and crimp the edges to seal. Brush the pastry with beaten egg.

Bake the tartlets for 25 minutes or until the pastry is cooked underneath and golden brown on top.

Rhubarb meringue pies

Makes: 4

Preparation time: **1 hour**

Cooking time: **28 minutes**

Ingredients

100 g / 3 ½ oz / ½ cup butter, cubed

200 g / 7 oz / 1 ⅓ cups plain
(all purpose) flour

600 g / 1 lb 5 ½ oz / 3 cups rhubarb stems

100 g / 3 ½ oz ½ cup caster
(superfine) sugar

For the meringue

4 large egg whites

110g / 4 oz / ½ cup caster
(superfine) sugar

Method

Preheat the oven to 200°C (180°C fan) / 400F / gas 6.

Rub the butter into the flour, then add just enough cold water to bind. Chill for 30 minutes, then roll out on a floured surface. Use the pastry to line a 23 cm (9 in) loose-bottomed tart tin and prick it with a fork.

Line the pastry with cling film and fill with baking beans or rice then bake for 10 minutes. Remove the cling film and beans and cook for another 8 minutes to crisp.

While the pastry is cooking, put the rhubarb and sugar in a saucepan with 4 tbsp of water. Cover and poach gently for 6 minutes or until the rhubarb is just tender. Drain well and divide between the pastry cases.

Whisk the egg whites until stiff, then gradually add the sugar and whisk until the mixture is thick and shiny. Spoon the meringue into a piping bag fitted with a large star nozzle and pipe a big swirl on top of each tart.

Return the tarts to the oven to bake for 10 minutes or until golden brown.

Raspberry and ricotta lattice tart

Serves: 6

Preparation time: 45 minutes

Cooking time: 45 minutes

Ingredients

2 large eggs

100 g / 3 ½ oz / ½ cup caster
   (superfine) sugar

450 g / 1 lb / 2 ½ cups fresh ricotta

100 ml / 3 ½ fl. oz / ½ cup double
   (heavy) cream

1 tsp vanilla extract

200 g / 7 oz / 1 ⅓ cups raspberries

For the pastry

400 g / 14 oz / 2 ⅔ cups plain
   (all purpose) flour

200 g / 7 oz / ¾ cup butter,
   cubed and chilled

1 large egg, beaten

Method

Preheat the oven to 160°C (140°C fan) / 325F / gas 3.

Sieve the flour into a mixing bowl, then rub in the butter until the mixture resembles fine breadcrumbs. Stir in just enough cold water to bring the pastry together into a pliable dough. Chill for 30 minutes.

Roll out the pastry on a floured surface and use it to line a large rectangular baking tin. Trim off the edges with a fluted pastry wheel and reserve the offcuts.

Whisk the eggs and sugar together for 3 minutes or until thick, then whisk in the ricotta, cream and vanilla extract. Fold in two thirds of the raspberries, then pour the mixture into the pastry case and level the top. Scatter over the remaining raspberries.

Re-roll the pastry trimmings and cut them into strips with the pastry wheel. Lay them over the top of the tart in a lattice pattern, then brush the top with beaten egg.

Bake the tart for 45 minutes or until a skewer inserted into the centre comes out clean and the pastry is cooked underneath.

Apple frangipane tart

Serves: **8**

Preparation time: **45 minutes**

Cooking time: **45 minutes**

Ingredients

110 g / 4 oz / ½ cup butter, cubed
  and chilled
225 g / 8 oz / 1 ½ cups plain
  (all purpose) flour
3 eating apples, peeled, cored and very
  thinly sliced

For the frangipane

55 g / 2 oz / ½ cup ground almonds
55 g / 2 oz / ¼ cup caster (superfine)
  sugar
55 g / 2 oz / ¼ cup butter, softened
1 large egg
1 tsp almond essence

Method

Rub the butter into the flour, then add just enough cold water to bind the mixture together into a pliable dough. Roll out the pastry on a floured surface and use it to line a 23 cm (9 in) round tart case. Leave the pastry to chill the fridge for 30 minutes.

Preheat the oven to 200°C (180°C fan) / 400F / gas 6.

Line the pastry case with cling film and fill it with baking beans, then bake for 15 minutes.

To make the frangipane, combine the ground almonds, sugar, butter, egg and almond essence in a bowl and whisk together for 2 minutes or until smooth.

When the pastry case is ready, remove the cling film and baking beans and layer up the apple slices and frangipane mixture inside.

Bake for 30 minutes or until a skewer inserted comes out clean. Serve hot or cold.

Strawberry and chocolate meringue pie

Serves: **8**

Preparation time: **1 hour**

Cooking time: **28 minutes**

Ingredients

100 g / 3 ½ oz / ½ cup butter, cubed

200 g / 7 oz / 1 ⅓ cups plain
   (all purpose) flour

2 tbsp unsweetened cocoa powder

4 tbsp strawberry jam (jelly)

4 large egg whites

100 g / 3 ½ oz / ½ cup caster
   (superfine) sugar

150 g / 5 ½ oz / 1 cup strawberries

icing (confectioners') sugar for dusting

Method

Preheat the oven to 200°C (180°C fan) / 400F / gas 6.

Rub the butter into the flour and cocoa, then add just enough cold water to bind. Chill for 30 minutes then roll out on a floured surface. Use the pastry to line a 24 cm (9 in) loose-bottomed tart tin and prick it with a fork.

Line the pastry with cling film and fill with baking beans or rice then bake for 10 minutes. Remove the cling film and beans and cook for another 8 minutes to crisp. Spoon the jam into the pastry case.

Whisk the egg whites until stiff, then gradually add the sugar and whisk until the mixture is thick and shiny. Spoon the meringue on top of the jam and smooth with a palette knife. Return to the oven for 10 minutes to lightly brown the top.

Leave to cool a little, then arrange the strawberries on top and dust with icing sugar.

Apple and blueberry frangipane pie

Serves: 8

Preparation time: 45 minutes

Cooking time: 30 minutes

Ingredients

200 g / 7 oz / 1 cup butter, cubed
    and chilled
400 g / 14 oz / 2 ⅔ cups plain
    (all purpose) flour
2 large bramley apples, peeled, cored
    and diced
150 g / 5 ½ oz / 1 cup blueberries
3 tbsp sultanas

For the frangipane

100 g / 3 ½ oz / 1 cup ground almonds
100 g / 3 ½ oz / ½ cup caster
    (superfine) sugar
100 g / 3 ½ oz / ½ cup butter, softened
2 large eggs
1 tsp almond essence

Method

Rub the butter into the flour, then add just enough cold water to bind the mixture together into a pliable dough. Roll out the pastry on a floured surface and use it to line a deep 23 cm (9 in) spring-form cake tin. Leave the pastry to chill in the fridge for 30 minutes.

Preheat the oven to 200°C (180°C fan) / 400F / gas 6.

To make the frangipane, combine the ground almonds, sugar, butter, egg and almond essence in a bowl and whisk together for 2 minutes or until smooth.

Mix the apples with the blueberries and sultanas, then layer them up with the frangipane inside the pastry case.

Fold the edges of the pastry over the top, then bake for 30 minutes or until a skewer inserted comes out clean. Serve hot or cold.

Pear frangipane tart

Serves: 6

Preparation time: **20 minutes**

Cooking time: **30 minute**

Ingredients

450 g / 1 lb / 2 cups ready-to-roll puff pastry

75 g / 2 ½ oz / ¾ cup ground almonds

75 g / 2 ½ oz / ⅓ cup butter, softened

75 g / 2 ½ oz / ⅓ cup caster
   (superfine) sugar

1 large egg

1 tbsp plain (all purpose) flour

400 g / 14 oz/ 2 cups of pear halves in
   syrup, drained

Method

Preheat the oven to 200°C (180°C fan) / 400F / gas 6.

Roll out the pastry on a floured surface and use it to line a rectangular baking tin.

Whisk together the almonds, butter, sugar, eggs, thyme and flour until smoothly whipped, then spoon the mixture into the pastry case.

Arrange the pear halves on top, then bake in the oven for 30 minutes or until the frangipane is cooked through in the centre.

Apple and walnut pie

Serves: 6

Preparation time: 20 minutes

Cooking time: 40 minutes

Ingredients

2 Bramley apples, peeled, cored and
  thinly sliced
100 g / 3 ½ oz / ⅔ cup walnut halves
1 lemon, zest finely grated
1 tsp cornflour (cornstarch)
2 tbsp caster (superfine) sugar

For the pastry

200 g / 7 oz / 1 cup butter, cubed
  and chilled
400 g / 14 oz / 2 ⅔ cups plain
  (all purpose) flour
1 egg, beaten

Method

Preheat the oven to 200°C (180°C fan) / 400F / gas 6.

To make the pastry, rub the butter into the flour, then
add just enough cold water to bind the mixture together
into a pliable dough. Roll out half of the pastry on a
floured surface and use it to line a shallow pie dish.

Toss the apples with the walnuts, lemon zest, cornflour
and sugar, then pack the mixture into the pastry case.

Roll out the rest of the pastry and lay it over the top.
Trim away any excess, then roll the edges in and crimp
to seal. Make a hole in the centre for the steam to
escape.

Brush the top of the pie with beaten egg, then bake
for 40 minutes or until the pastry is cooked through
underneath and golden brown on top.

Marmalade Breton tart

Serves: 6

Preparation time: 15 minutes

Cooking time: 40–45 minutes

Ingredients

250 g / 9 oz / 1 ¼ cups butter, cubed

250 g / 9 oz / 1 ⅔ cups plain
(all purpose) flour

250 g / 9 oz / 1 ¼ cups caster
(superfine) sugar

5 large egg yolks

175 g / 6 oz / ½ cup marmalade

icing (confectioners') sugar for dusting

Method

Preheat the oven to 180°C (160°C fan) / 350F / gas 4 and butter a 20 cm (8 in) round loose-bottomed cake tin.

Rub the butter into the flour with a pinch of salt, then stir in the sugar.

Beat the egg yolks and stir them into the dry ingredients.

Bring the mixture together into a soft dough and divide it in two. Put half in the freezer for 10 minutes. Press the other half into the bottom of the cake tin to form an even layer. Spread the marmalade on top.

Coarsely grate the other half of the dough over the top and press down lightly.

Bake the tart for 40–45 minutes or until golden brown and cooked through.

Cool completely before unmoulding and dusting with icing sugar.

Lemon and passion fruit tart

Serves: **8**

Preparation time: **45 minutes**

Cooking time: **50 minutes**

Ingredients

4 passion fruits, halved

2 lemons, juiced

175 g / 6 oz / ¾ cup caster
(superfine) sugar

2 tsp cornflour (cornstarch)

4 large eggs, beaten

225 ml / 8 fl. oz / ¾ cup double
(heavy) cream

For the pastry

100 g / 3 ½ oz / ½ cup butter, cubed

200 g / 7 oz / 1 ⅓ cups plain
(all purpose) flour

50 g / 1 ¾ oz / ¼ cup caster
(superfine) sugar

1 large egg, beaten

Method

Preheat the oven to 200°C (180°C fan) / 400F / gas 6.

To make the pastry, rub the butter into the flour and
sugar, then add enough beaten egg to bind it into a
pliable dough.

Wrap the dough in cling film and chill for 30 minutes,
then roll out on a floured surface. Use the pastry to line
a 23 cm (9 in) loose-bottomed tart tin and trim the
edges. Prick the pastry with a fork, line with cling film,
and fill with baking beans or rice.

Bake the pastry case for 10 minutes then remove the
cling film and baking beans and cook for another
8 minutes to crisp.

Reduce the oven temperature to 160°C (140°C fan) /
325F / gas 3.

Scoop the passion fruit seeds and pulp into a bowl and
stir in the lemon juice, sugar and cornflour to dissolve,
then whisk in the eggs and cream.

Pour the mixture into the pastry case and bake for
30 minutes or until just set in the centre.

Leave to cool completely before serving.

Index

Index